The above advertisement is reproduced by courtesy of
Mr Chris White from his collection at Loughborough

to teachers and parents

This is a LADYBIRD LEADER book, one of a series specially produced to meet the very real need for carefully planned *first information books* that instantly attract enquiring minds and stimulate reluctant readers.

The subject matter and vocabulary have been selected with expert assistance, and the brief and simple text is printed in large, clear type.

Children's questions are anticipated and facts presented in a logical sequence. Where possible, the books show what happened in the past and what is relevant today.

Special artwork has been commissioned to set a standard rarely seen in books for this reading age and at this price.

Full colour illustrations are on all 48 pages to give maximum impact and provide the extra enrichment that is the aim of all Ladybird Leaders.

Acknowledgment

The publishers wish to acknowledge the help given by the Nestlé Company Ltd in the preparation of this book, and also their permission to reproduce the photograph of a vending machine, on the inside front cover.

A Ladybird Leader

chocolate
and cocoa

by Michael Smith
with illustrations by B. H. Robinson

Ladybird Books Ltd Loughborough 1977

Which do you like best?

Nearly everyone likes chocolate,
and it is easy to carry
wherever we go.

Do you have a favourite kind?

On a cold night nothing is nicer
than a mug of hot frothy cocoa
or drinking chocolate.

It tastes good and warms us up.

Cocoa pods

The cocoa you enjoy so much
comes from a pod
which grows on the trunk of a tree.

The tree grows
in the hot wet forests
of South America and Africa.

The first cocoa drink

Men who lived in the Amazon forests
of South America
hundreds of years ago
knew that a good drink could be made
from the beans they found
inside the pod.

The Aztecs drank chocolate

In the great cities of the Aztecs
(in the land that is now Mexico),
chocolate was the favourite drink
of the people.

Montezuma, their Emperor,
gave his guests cups of chocolate
flavoured with vanilla seed.

The drink was whisked up until frothy
and drunk from gold cups.

Bartering with cocoa

In parts of America
the valuable beans were used
instead of money
to buy things people needed.

The beans could be exchanged
for cloth, or tools or even animals.

The old words

The Aztec name for the drink
was CHOCOLATL.

The tree was called CACAUATL.

It is from these old words
that we get *chocolate* and *cocoa*.

11

Cocoa comes to Europe

When Hernando Cortez
conquered Mexico in 1521,
he took the secret of cocoa
back to Spain with him.

Smuggling cocoa

The Spaniards tried
to keep the secret to themselves
but the news soon spread.

Smugglers risked great danger
to deliver cargoes
of the precious beans
to other parts of Europe.

Chocolate houses

Soon 'chocolate houses'
were to be found in London.

People met in them to talk together
and to enjoy the new drink.

The beans were very expensive,
so only the rich could afford
to buy the drink.

In 1664 Samuel Pepys,
the famous writer,
wrote in his diary,
"Went to Mr. Bland's
and there drank my morning draft
of good chocollatte."

15

Where cocoa came from

Cocoa seeds were taken
from the Amazon forests
to grow in other parts of the world.

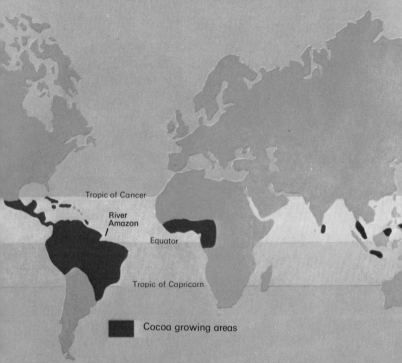

Tropic of Cancer

River
Amazon

Equator

Tropic of Capricorn

Cocoa growing areas

The trees will only grow
in countries which are always hot
and have much rain.

Careful cultivation

Cocoa farmers in Ghana
look after their seedlings
very carefully.

They often plant them
under taller trees which give shade.

The young trees grow best
in rich soil.

The cocoa tree

When the tree is fully grown
it is between 6 and 10 metres tall.

It does not have many branches.

The flowers

When it is four or five years old
small pale pink flowers grow
in clusters on the trunk
and on the branches.

Some of the hundreds of flowers
will produce seed pods.

The pods ripen

The pods swell up
until they are
about 15 centimetres long.

As they ripen, their colour changes
from green to golden yellow.

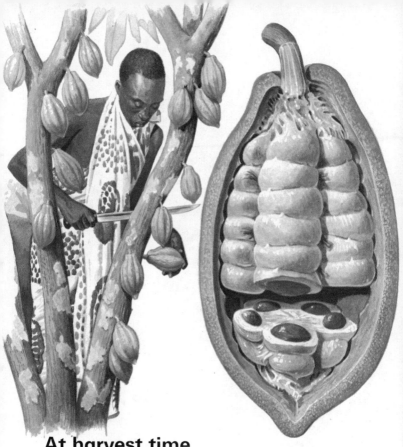

At harvest time

Men cut the pods from the trees
with *machetes* (long sharp knives).
Each pod has
about forty purple beans
set in a white pulp.

The village
at harvest time

Women and young girls
carry the pods back to the village
in baskets which they balance
on their heads.

In the village
men break open the pods
with mallets or knives.

They take great care not to damage
the precious beans.

Scooping out the beans

Girls scoop out the beans and pulp.
They build these into mounds
which they cover
with plantain leaves.

Fermentation

During the next few days
the beans begin to ferment
in the heat under the leaves.

Now the real chocolate flavour
starts to develop.

Drying the beans

When the watery pulp
has drained away
the beans are spread out
in the sun to dry.

They have changed colour
from purple to brown.

They can be covered up quickly
if it looks like rain.

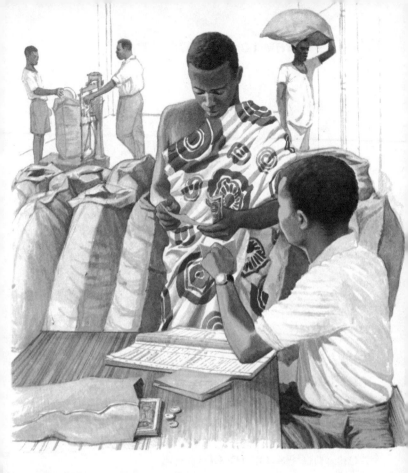

Selling the crop

Soon the beans are dry enough
to be put into sacks
and taken to the *buying station*
where the farmer sells his crop.

The journey to the factory

In some countries
the sacks may be 'head-loaded'
to the nearest road or railway.

In other parts of the world
the beans may be carried
on mules or in canoes.

A long sea voyage

At the port the heavy sacks
are lifted into the holds
of the cargo ships.

The ship will take them
on the long sea voyage
to factories in other countries.

By surf-boat to the ship

In Ghana at one time
the sacks were taken
through huge waves by *surf-boat*.

The sea was too shallow
for the cargo ship to come closer.

Where cocoa is grown

Most of the world's cocoa
is grown in West Africa,
on the Ivory Coast
and in Ghana and Nigeria.

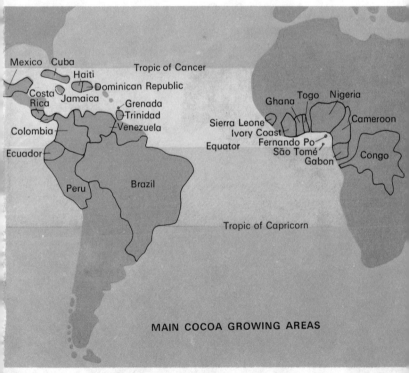

MAIN COCOA GROWING AREAS

Some comes from Brazil
and other parts of America.

The first eating chocolate

Although cocoa beans
have been used to make a drink
for hundreds of years,
chocolate to eat was not popular
until about 1850.

Cleaning and roasting

When the beans reach the factory
by road, rail or canal,
they are cleaned.

Then they are roasted
for about an hour
in a large rotating oven.

cocoa nib

Winnowing and grinding

After the beans are roasted
it is easy to remove the *husk* or skin
from the pure cocoa *nib*.

This process is called *winnowing*.

The nib goes into a grinding mill
where it is turned into a thick paste
known as *mass*.

Cakes of cocoa

The mass has too much *cocoa-butter* in it to make good cocoa.

Some of this has to be squeezed out in a powerful press.

The press makes a circular *cake* of hard cocoa.

35

Crushing

The cakes
are crushed
to a fine powder
in a crushing mill.

The powder is sieved
so that no lumps get into the tins.

The labelled tins are sent
to your local shop.

Mixing

Plain dark eating chocolate
is made from the mass,
cocoa-butter and white sugar.

These ingredients are mixed up
in a machine called a *mélangeur.*
(*say* may-lon-jer)

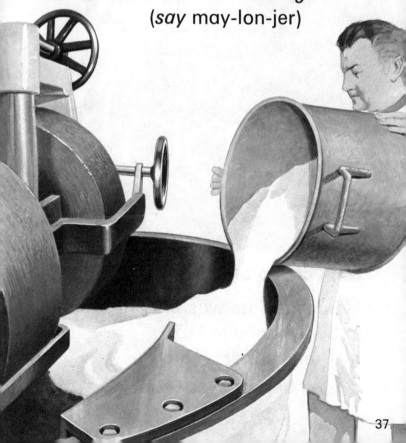

Milk chocolate

Milk chocolate was first invented
in Switzerland in 1876,
by Daniel Peter.

It soon became very popular.

Condensed milk

Fresh milk does not mix easily
with the fats in the cocoa-butter,
so it must be *condensed*
before it is added to the cocoa mass.

Conching

Heavy rollers push the mixture
backwards and forwards
for many hours
until it is really smooth.

This process is called *conching*.

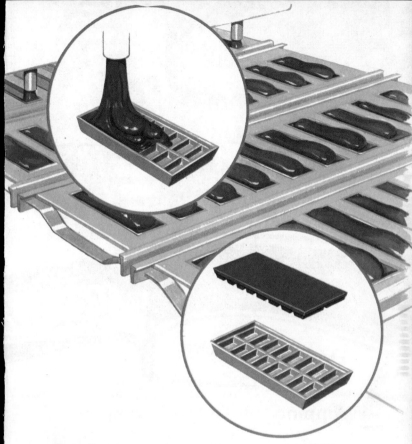

Setting

The smooth liquid chocolate
is poured into polished moulds.

These travel on a conveyor belt
through a cold room
so that the chocolate can set.

Wrapping

Wrapping machines cover
the blocks with silver paper,
which is thin aluminium foil.

This keeps the chocolate
in perfect condition.

The wrapper is put on last of all.

All shapes and sizes

You can buy blocks of chocolate
in rectangles, circles, and triangles,
as well as in animal shapes.

Fillings

Many different foods can be mixed with chocolate.

Almonds, hazelnuts, Brazil nuts, raisins and cherries are all used.

Can you think of any more?

Many other flavours are used
as the fillings for chocolates —
lime, pineapple, coconut,
strawberry, ginger or nougat.

Liquid chocolate is poured
over the filling to coat the centre.

Covering biscuits

Chocolate is used
to cover different kinds
of biscuit and wafer.

The flavour of chocolate blends well
with many other foods.

Flavouring with chocolate

Chocolate or cocoa is used
to flavour many of the foods
we like best.

Have you ever helped
to make a chocolate cake?

The right amount
of cocoa powder
is mixed in
before the cake is baked.

From factory to shop

Many people help
to get the chocolate and cocoa
from the factory to the shops.

The cartons of cocoa or chocolate
go by road and rail.

All different kinds

In your sweetshop
there are so many kinds of sweets
that it is often difficult to choose.

Other uses of the cocoa pod

Even those parts of the cocoa pod
not used for making chocolate
are made into other useful things.

The shell is made into animal food
and the cocoa-butter is used
to make lipsticks and perfume.

Don't drop your wrappers!

Please don't drop
your chocolate wrappers
on the ground.

Help to keep our streets tidy
and our countryside beautiful
by using a litter basket.

51

Index